A PRESENCE IN THE DARK:

Finding Hope in Death

By

BRAD RILEY

*To Gail,
May these words be a blessing to your journey!
Shalom
Brad Riley*

Copyright © 2017 Brad Riley

All rights reserved.

ISBN-13: 978-1976483318
Printed in the United States of America
MSC Press
Cover design: Brad Riley

All Scripture quotations, unless otherwise noted are from the Revised Standard Version Bible, copyright © 1946, 1952 and 1971 the Division of Christian Education of the National Council of the Churches of Christ in the United States of America. Used by permission. All rights reserved.

Scriptures marked KJV are taken from the KING JAMES VERSION (KJV): KING JAMES VERSION, public domain.

Scriptures marked NLT are taken from the HOLY BIBLE, NEW LIVING TRANSLATION (NLT): Scriptures taken from the HOLY BIBLE, NEW LIVING TRANSLATION, Copyright© 1996, 2004, 2007 by Tyndale House Foundation. Used by permission of Tyndale House Publishers, Inc., Carol Stream, Illinois 60188. All rights reserved. Used by permission.

Scriptures marked ESV are taken from the THE HOLY BIBLE, ENGLISH STANDARD VERSION (ESV): Scriptures taken from THE HOLY BIBLE, ENGLISH STANDARD VERSION ® Copyright© 2001 by Crossway, a publishing ministry of Good News Publishers. Used by permission.

Scriptures marked NAS are taken from the NEW AMERICAN STANDARD (NAS): Scripture taken from the NEW AMERICAN STANDARD BIBLE®, copyright© 1960, 1962, 1963, 1968, 1971, 1972, 1973, 1975, 1977, 1995 by The Lockman Foundation. Used by permission.

Scriptures marked NIV are taken from the NEW INTERNATIONAL VERSION (NIV): Scripture taken from THE HOLY BIBLE, NEW INTERNATIONAL VERSION ®. Copyright© 1973, 1978, 1984, 2011 by Biblica, Inc.™. Used by permission of Zondervan

IN MEMORY OF

Uncle Forrest

... who stood in our lives as a gentle giant of a man exemplifying to my wife and I the beauty of Christlikeness in his work, family, service to the church, and perhaps most importantly for how he faced death with dignity, humility, love, and hope... the hope of knowing that death was not the end of his life, but rather the beginning.
May his memory be eternal.

Forrest W. Newlin
1928 - 1997

and

Charlie

...my brother in whom I saw so much love and goodness as he saw life for its simple beauty, and who saw so much of God in His beautiful creation; the mountains, lakes and streams called out to him.
May his memory be eternal.

Charles E. Riley
1950 - 2011

CONTENTS

Foreword

Introduction

1   Our Common Denominator   Pg 9

2   Why Life?   Pg 17

3   Never Alone   Pg 31

4   The Beauty of the Body   Pg 45

5   Incarnational Living   Pg 57

6   Removing the Shroud   Pg 71

7   Finding Hope   Pg 83

8   Epilogue   Pg 93

"The fear of death follows from the fear of life. A man who lives fully is prepared to die at any time."

Mark Twain

"Remembering that I'll be dead soon is the most important tool I've ever encountered to help me make the big choices in life. Because almost everything - all external expectations, all pride, all fear of embarrassment or failure - these things just fall away in the face of death, leaving only what is truly important."

Steve Jobs

FOREWORD

It has been a true privilege and honor to co-minister though the years with Brad Riley. As a funeral professional, I have had the opportunity to work with a countless number of clergy throughout my 25-year career. Brad certainly stands out as one of the best. His heart for the Lord translates into a heart for people – all people. Regardless of their religious background or lack thereof, economic status or even race, I have watched him connect with and positively impact the lives of those he serves.

All of us at Cozine Memorial Group have confidently recommended him for years to families that do not have a pastor or church of their own. We know without a doubt that these families will be cared for and ministered to by someone who genuinely cares for them.

Each year the National Funeral Directors Association holds its annual International Convention and Expo in a major U.S. City. More than 6,000 people from every facet of the funeral service profession attend this event. They gather from all over the United States and throughout the world. Each year, it's the responsibility of the NFDA president to select the chaplain for the convention. I am honored and privileged to name Brad Riley, to the role of the 2017 NFDA Convention Chaplain in Boston, Massachusetts. I can't think of a better person to represent clergy at this international funeral event.

W. Ashley Cozine, CFSP, CPC, CCO
President, Cozine Memorial Group
2016 - 2017 NFDA President

INTRODUCTION

It's been said that there are only two things in this world that are a given – death and taxes. I'm not totally convinced on the taxes. I suppose it's possible for some group of people somewhere to decide everybody would pay his own way in life and there would be no taxing of the people, although it seems highly unlikely. I'm pretty sure that was the situation in the ancient world of Adam and Eve and Noah.

However, while I'm not really sure when and where the first taxing of people began, I am sure about physical death; it began with Cain killing Abel, and it's the destiny of every one of us. Actually, I must correct myself. History and the Bible tells us that at least two, possibly three persons were taken up into Heaven without a physical death, Enoch and Elijah, and some would add the Blessed Virgin Mary. Clearly they were very special people.

When most things become common place in our world we tend to get used to them. But not death. Death is the hardest thing we experience in life, and I hope we never get used to it. Getting used to death would be the ultimate devaluing of human life. I believe every human life is sacred, for all carry within them the image and breath of our Creator God. Every human life deserves to be mourned, for it is as the Psalmist said comparing humanity to the flowers of the field…

> *For the wind passeth over it, and it is gone; and the place thereof shall know it no more.*
> Psalm 103:16 KJV

Many things in life bring us pain and sorrow, but rarely are they as deep and profound as death. I'm aware that there is such horror and terror in this dark world that can produce such pain so as to cause the suffering one to beg for death. I pray such pain is not so for you or your loved ones. I pray that it will become less and less upon the earth as the kingdom of God is restored more and more moving us toward the end of all things…the peaceable kingdom. When death comes, we're never quite ready for it. Even when our loved one suffered greatly with an emaciating disease, and we had to endure their wasting away before our very eyes, we're still not quite ready for that final word, that final embrace.

So what can I speak into this universal pain that hasn't been said by someone before? Maybe nothing new, but I pray reading these thoughts will bring the incomparable comfort of God closer to you than ever before, and perhaps for just a time as this, as some of you are experiencing the greatest pain of your life as you face this great destroyer that is called death.

Upon seeing the immense suffering of the people of Israel at the hands of their captors in the Babylonian captivity, God speaks through the prophet Jeremiah the very words we are tempted to ask of Him…

> *For the wound of the daughter of my people is my heart wounded, I mourn, and dismay has taken hold on me. Is there no balm in Gilead? Is there no physician there? Why then has the health of the daughter of my people not been restored?*

Jeremiah 8:21-22

Another of the prophets of Israel said it this way… "*O LORD, how long shall I cry for help, and thou wilt not hear? Or cry to thee "Violence!" and thou wilt not save?*" Habbakuk 1:2

We've all called out to God for help and healing only to feel like our cries fell on deaf ears. In acknowledging that we don't understand why, perhaps we can now open our hearts to say with the Psalmist… *"Make me to know thy ways, O LORD; teach me thy paths."* Psalm 25:4

As you read this book, I pray you will see a greater vision of God than you've ever seen. Instead of asking God "Why" or "How long?" as the prophets did; I want us to look at life from a completely different paradigm – to see the blessing of living. We'll look into the ancient ways of God's people and see things that may be new to you. We'll look to the example of the incarnational life of Jesus Christ and consider how we too may live in such ways that speak life and hope in to the lives of hurting people.

I also pray that as you read this book you'll realize that no matter how dark things are in your life, and no matter how lonely you feel…you're not alone. The truth is our loved ones who've departed life as we know it are still very much alive and aware of our journey. In fact, they're more alive than us. They've crossed out of death and into life… life as it was always meant to be.

Most important of all, I pray that as you read this book you will find a new sense of hope: a hope that never disappoints, a hope that is beyond us in and of ourselves, a hope that is not only possible through Jesus Christ, but that *is* your promise in Him.

I don't guarantee that you'll agree with everything I say, but if you keep an open mind and hear the love in which I offer these thoughts; I promise you will find a presence in the dark who will bring a comfort this world can't and hope for the future… hope even in the face of death.

In Christ's Merciful Service,

Brad Riley

A PRESENCE IN THE DARK

> "The snares of death encompassed me; the pangs of Sheol laid hold on me; I suffered distress and anguish."
>
> -Psalm 116:3

1

OUR COMMON DENOMINATOR

They tried to look like they were happy to see me, but I wasn't buying it. After nine days in Guatemala I really thought my family would be happier to see me. I was afraid to let myself think of what news they had for me. It was about 7 o'clock in the evening on Sunday July 10, 2011 and my plane had just landed. I was traveling back from a "Work and Witness" trip with a team from my church. We'd just spent 10 days building a home for a pastor who was living in a one room hut with mud floors.

The day I left for Guatemala, my oldest brother Charlie was facing open heart surgery. Earlier that week he had a major heart attack while at work. It looked bad. I didn't want to leave him but as Associate Pastor of our church, I was going along as the chaplain for the trip; they definitely weren't taking me along for my knowledge of building, that was Charlie's gift.

He was 10 and a half years older than me. When I was

a kid I watched him tear down the motor of a '55 Chevy and put it back together. I was amazed. He was only in high school at the time. How could he know so much about tearing things apart and fixing them?

We knew his heart was damaged pretty badly. The echo-cardiogram showed the left atrium was about the size of a grapefruit which is pretty bad when you consider your whole heart should only be about the size of a human fist. Surely he had more time left with us. Charlie was a strong, hard-working guy. He was the head of maintenance for our hometown of Newton, Kansas.

We knew Charlie would have the surgery and recover. We just knew it; our faith told us so. Sure he would have to change his lifestyle. He would most likely have to retire early, which would be hard for him, but he could do it. He could do anything he put his mind to. It wouldn't be so bad. Now he could spend more time with his grandkids. Everything was going to be okay. After all, as a pastor, I said that to countless families in waiting rooms as they awaited news of their loved ones who were in surgery.

My brother wasn't one to go the doctor. In fact, his last check-up had been 15 years prior. He just always seemed strong to us. I never really thought to ask him if he was keeping up with his health; besides, he would have told me to mind my own business – he was okay.

But he wasn't okay. Apparently he had lived for several years with a leaky left Atrial valve. When left unattended, a leaky valve eventually causes blood to pool in the atrium, instead of emptying into the ventricle where it can be pumped out to the body. Charlie's had been pooling for a long time causing his Atrium to swell like a water balloon.

As they wheeled Charlie down the hallway to surgery, our family gathered around the gurney and held hands. I quoted a scripture, put my hand on his forehead and prayed a prayer for healing. Then, I told him I loved him and said *"I'll see you when I get back from Guatemala!"*

As Charlie went into surgery, I hurried off to the airport. I was so thankful his surgery was scheduled early in the morning so I could be there to pray with him before I left. I never saw my brother alive again. He died nine days later, just three hours before my plane landed back in Wichita. All of a sudden death was painfully real to me.

As my wife Rhonda, and daughter Brooke, looked at me with bittersweet eyes in the airport terminal that evening, I knew something was wrong. Surrounded by a group of people from my church who had gathered to greet the team, my family kissed me and told me they were happy to see me, and they were, but their heart was also breaking knowing they had to tell me the news of Charlie's passing. They prayed all day that Charlie would be able to hold on so I could see him one last time, but he couldn't. His time had come…as it will for all of us, and when it does, there's nothing we can do to change the outcome.

Life, it seems, had reached its lowest common denominator. There was nothing more to divide into, for Charlie. No machinery could keep his heart beating for one more minute. The breath of life God imparted to him had lasted for 60 years, 328 days, and about 16 hours… 37 days short of his 61st birthday.

I was never good at math but it seems to me the analogy of a common denominator is a good metaphor for death. For those who are also challenged by math, a denominator is the bottom number of a fraction, (yes I had to look that up to be sure). Each day of life is kind of like a fraction; a part of the whole. If you'll allow me to substitute a *thing* in place of a number, then there is one common *thing* that divides into every life – death.

> *You saw me before I was born. Every day of my life was recorded in your book. Every moment was laid out before a single day had passed.*
>
> -Psalm 139:16 NLT

Death is the one thing all living beings have in common. Regardless of race, creed, ethnicity, or social status, we all die. It's as Hank Hannegraaff, host of the radio program, *The Bible Answer Man,* often says, "The death ratio is still one per person," yet for something as common as death we still don't know much about it. Until we experience it for ourselves it remains aloof. We realize it happens and we care about those to whom it happens, but it's always something others are going through – until it's our turn.

When death strikes close to us it's then we realize how little we know about it…except that it hurts. Death hurts like no other pain in the world. It is without a doubt the hardest thing we experience as humans. We're left feeling numb with many questions and few answers. How do we face something we know so little about? What happens after we die? Is there life after death?

Religion has been trying to answer those questions since time began and the first person died. There are many religions in the world and each of them tries to answer those questions in their own way. Everyone has some kind of faith even if it's only in themselves. We're all seeking answers to questions about death whether we realize it or not. When we seek answers about the meaning of life we can't help but seek answers about death too that ultimately bring up more questions about faith. After all… life, death, and faith can't be separated.

> *Faith consists in being vitally concerned with that ultimate reality to which I give the symbolical name of God. Whoever reflects earnestly on the meaning of life is on the verge of an act of faith.*
> -Paul Tillich; 20th Century American Philosopher

As a Christian minister, I felt I should understand all this stuff about death better than I did. With my brother's passing, I came face to face with some real doubts. Not doubts about the existence of God. I wasn't on the verge of losing my faith as I've seen happen to some. Rather, they were more like doubts of purpose. If I couldn't find the answers to the big questions about life and death, then who could? Shouldn't ministers know these things? That seemed arrogant but I didn't intend it to be arrogant since I honestly felt that way.

As I began to work through my own grief, what I found was that most of my colleagues were in the same boat. They were men and women of faith; they could teach all the Christian doctrines about Heaven and Hell, but when it came to really knowing how to make sense of death they were just as stumped as me.

So, I too entered the valley of the shadow of death. Over time I began to realize we don't enter the valley when death comes. We enter the valley when we're born. Our entire life is the valley of the shadow of death. But that's actually good news…it's a valley not a canyon. Valleys are open at both ends not closed like canyons.

Life is not a dead-end road. There is hope and there are answers about the meaning of life and death, but I'm getting ahead of myself since I'll speak more of that in later chapters. For now it's important for us to see that we all share in a common denominator. We're all human beings of equal value to God, and we're all going to die someday.

Well, that doesn't exactly seem like an upbeat thought to end a chapter on does it? In fact, it is an upbeat ending. If I could promise you there's nothing to fear in death, and, in fact, you can look forward to it; would you read on to see how? I hope so.

We're all on a journey through the valley of the shadow of death. Like all journeys, it's a lot better when we can share it with someone. The more we do life together; the more grace we find in death together. I know that's a strange thought… doing death together, but think about it. The only thing worse than facing death is facing death alone.

So, how do we face death together? By being there for each other in life. Ultimately, I was able to face my brother's death in a healthier way, not because I was a Christian minister who was trained to handle death experiences, but because I had the love and support of family and friends; even though they didn't have the answers to all my questions; they were there for me, and I was there for them.

Do I have it all figured out and that's why I'm writing this book? Absolutely not. But, I have figured out a few things. I believe what we look for in life will help shape what we look for in death. Life is too special to just end abruptly in death. Life is too great a gift to be so one dimensional as being only physical.

What about the spiritual component of life? What's it all about? Could it be that when we discover the spiritual meaning to life it helps us face death and having to say goodbye physically to our loved ones with hope? Let's seek that answer together as we ponder the really big question of life – not why death but why life?

> *"Return, O my soul, to your rest; for the LORD has dealt bountifully with you. For thou hast delivered my soul from death, my eyes from tears, my feet from stumbling;"*
>
> Psalm 116:7-8

2

WHY LIFE?

The 1966 award winning song writing duo, Burt Bacharach and Hal David, posed the greatest question we can ask in their title song to the movie "Alfie"…

What's it all about, Alfie? Is it just for the moment we live? What's it all about, when you sort it out, Alfie?[1]

Is it just for the moment we live? That's a great follow up question. Everything in me screams the answer is NO! We don't live just for the moment; we live for eternity! I'll expand my thoughts on eternity more in chapter three, but if we're to find real meaning to life in this world we need to begin by embracing the thought that this world isn't all there is.

---

[1] "Alfie"; Burt Bacharach - Hal David, Parlaphone (UK), Capitol Records (US), 1966

As you may have noticed by the obscure song reference, I'm kind of a modern philosophy nerd. You know? The kind of guy who not only loves to read the classic philosophers of the ages, but also thinks there's good philosophy in the lyrics of pop songs. I guess you could call me a "Pop Philosopher". As we seek the meaning of life, especially in light of the grief we experience in death, and before we try to understand death, let's listen to the words of sage philosophers, Jim Seals and Dash Crofts. "Dash", what a cool name. That guy was born to philosophize.

> *Life, so they say, is but a game and we let it slip away. Love, like the Autumn sun, should be dyin' but it's only just begun. Like the twilight in the road up ahead, they don't see just where we're goin'. And all the secrets of the Universe whisper in our ears, And all the years will come and go, takes us up, always up. We may never pass this way again. We may never pass this way again. We may never pass this way again.*[2]

I know you were singing those words instead of reading them, weren't you? It's ok. I was singing them as I typed. A wise man once said (I can't remember from whom or where I heard this) *"Music is like a platform for our souls to dance upon"*. Singing is actually a very ancient prayer language. In both, the Old Testament days and in the early Christian church, the

---

[2] "We May Never Pass This Way (Again)"; Jim **Seals - Dash Crofts,** Warner Bros. Records, 1973.

whole of worship services were sung. Some still sing their liturgies, like the Eastern Orthodox, for example. Modern Protestant worship styles are often filled with singing as well.

Why do we sing? Because singing is a deeper expression of the soul than speaking. An entire Christian worship service without any music is, well, boring. The only example of a worship service without music I can think of is the daily Mass in most Catholic churches. The only reason they cut out the music is to shorten the service to about a half hour allowing for people to come before or after work.

The truth is, God's people love to sing, except of course for everybody's grumpy old uncle who can't carry a tune in a bucket. He says he doesn't like or need to sing but deep in his heart I bet he wishes he could. In fact, in his heart I bet he is singing, even if it's just *"Mamas, don't let your babies grow up to be cowboys"*[3] while he's puttering around in his garage.

The Bible is filled with singing from beginning to end. The Book of Psalms is actually a song book full of prayers to be sung by God's people. Many of the psalms actually command us to sing. If you think that command was only for Old Testament believers, consider that St. Paul commanded the Ephesians to go about their daily lives *"...singing psalms and hymns and*

---

[3] "Mommas Don't Let Your Babies Grow Up to Be Cowboys; Ed Bruce - Patsy Bruce, United Artists, 1975.

spiritual songs among yourselves, and making music to the Lord in your hearts."[4]

Also, Psalm 96:1-2 commands us to sing:

Sing to the LORD a new song; Sing to the LORD, all the earth. Sing to the LORD, bless His name; Proclaim good tidings of His salvation from day to day.[5]

Do you have a song in your heart? You know, a subconscious tune that just bubbles up in your soul from day to day and time to time? Do you sometimes find yourself singing out loud when you're walking down the hallway at work or driving in your car? I know some people are more musical than others but having a song in your soul isn't about being musical; it's just there. I think most truly happy people have a song in their soul. Sometimes we don't know that about people because those who aren't particularly musical are afraid to let it out.

The problem with life is that when really tough times come they can knock the song right out of our soul. We lose all the wind in our sails and there just isn't any left with which to sing. Sadness takes over, and in the case of a loved one's death we begin to grieve. It's times like this we must remember that grief is not the enemy. It's okay to grieve. In fact, grieving is natural

---

[4] Ephesians 5:19, NLT

[5] Psalm 96:1-2, NLT

and therapeutic.

However, to many people with no faith in God life seems like a game. It seems like a game without a rule book that tells us how to play, a game without a strategy to win. And not just any game, but a cruel one at that. We're born. We grow up. We go to work. We live and then we die – or so it seems. There's no rhyme or reason to how long we live or how we die. We try our best at life, but sometimes, everything seems to go against us; it seems those tough times just keep coming.

Here's where we must begin; life must have meaning and purpose to help us through those tough times. There's no reason for us to exist if it doesn't. And, the toughest of times are when the ones we love the most die. Often, the toughness is aggravated by the way they die. In the process of grieving the loss of our loved one we grope for answers to why. Why did our loved one die? Why did he or she die a certain way? That question is particularly heavy when death comes by tragic circumstance, or seemingly out of time. Nothing seems fair. It's in those times where it just doesn't seem fair that we have to remember, life isn't fair. Nowhere in the world is it written that life is fair.

When we ask "Why" to all the above questions, we're really asking the wrong question. It's not "Why death?", but "Why life?". If we're going to make any sense of life, death, and grief we must come to realize that to live, no matter how long or under what circumstances, is the greatest privilege of all. To live in this world means we will live in the next world also. And, how we live in this world actually determines how we live in the next (more about that later in the book).

Life is so precious we instinctively want to preserve it at all cost, and well we should; it's the greatest of all God's gifts. When we lose sight of how precious life is we stop living and begin to just exist. So, why have we lost sight of just how precious life is? While this isn't a book about all the cultural problems of our day, I do want to mention that it seems to me the real problem with how we view life is found in our present culture of death.

We are a people way to pre-occupied with death. Perhaps this pre-occupation is because of the constant war that seems to rage somewhere on the planet. If WWII was the war to end all wars (as it was popularly referred to) it failed miserably. In less than a decade the world was embattled in Korea. In less than another decade there was the Vietnam conflict, and so on, and so on. It seems global conflict is unavoidable.

Then, as we approached the beginning of a new millennium, traditional waring between nations and armies gave way to the horrors of terrorism – a new global kind of war. But who are we kidding? War and terrorism have existed since the beginning of civilization and I suppose they will continue until Christ comes to usher in the next world. So the existence of war isn't the real cause for our current culture of death, but the increasingly terroristic nature of war is a frightening effect on a culture consumed with death.

If we really want to understand what's led to such a fascination with death we need look no further than our own households. The breakdown of the family unit is the number one contributing factor in this present culture of death; the present darkness that seems to be ever growing. Families were once a place of peace and safety. In 1970, only 12% of people between the ages of 35 and 44 (a strong child rearing age group) were not married. By 2009, fully one-third of the same group were not married. That's a significant increase. Today almost 1 in 3 persons' ages 35 – 44 are not married. Furthermore, when we look at the fact that by 2009 the birth rate to unmarried mothers rose to a whopping 41% we can begin to understand the alarming breakdown in families.[6]

There are many other statistics that can be noted and it doesn't take a rocket scientist to know there are adverse effects to such breakdowns in society, but this isn't a book about such problems; it's a book about finding hope in our present grief. If we're to begin making sense of life, especially in the context of facing death, then I think we have to acknowledge the changes around us.

Today, too many children grow up with a vastly

---

[6]http://www.nationalreview.com/article/367109/uncomfortable-truths-about-family-breakdown-michael-barone

different idea of what it means to have a safe and stable home life. If you're one of those statistics mentioned above you know what I mean. Hopefully, the home you grew up in was a safe place, full of love, even if you had just one parent. However, according to the numbers, chances are pretty good it wasn't.

Truthfully, when you add in the rapid decline of social mores that once protected children from too early of an exposure to things like sex and violence, what we're left with today is a generation with great anxiety. Life isn't what it was for previous generations; it doesn't offer the same opportunities for stability and advancement. Coupled with the rapid rise in terrorism, the world just isn't as safe as it once was. Today, it's not just adults who are doing the killing. Children are taking guns to school and killing other children. Things have definitely changed and changed for the worse.

Well, that's enough depressing thoughts. I want us to look at life today with both eyes open. I began this chapter asking you to change your question from why death, to why life? When we experience the death of a loved one, however death comes, the best thing we can do is remember their life. They lived and loved, even if only for a little while, and we got to love them back… even if only for a little while.

I want to repeat something I said in the beginning of the chapter. **The greatest privilege in the world is to be born.** To be born in this world means we will live in the next world also. The second greatest privilege in the world is to love. Life only makes sense when we experience love. Why? Because God is love and God is life, and to be born in this world, and to love another person is to experience the life of God. No matter how your life has turned out so far, even if you're lonely and don't feel loved, I want to assure you of one thing you can count on right now – **God loves you and it doesn't even matter if you love him back.**

When we realize that God is love and God is life, we can know that our being loved is not dependent on any other person. God loves everyone. Yes, that means you… especially you.

When we lose sight of how precious life is we stop living and begin to just exist

Grief has a way of stealing our emotions. The loss of a loved one creates a vacuum that can never be filled in the same way. Life suddenly feels like a great void. Things that used to bring us joy no longer do. It's important for us to realize that these feelings of emptiness are natural. In fact, they're unavoidable. Life is too precious to lose and not be missed, and missed greatly.

Psychologists tell us there are varying stages to grief. Not everyone goes through them the same. It's important to know that when the void left in the wake of death begins to take over, the worst thing we can do is deny our feelings. Instead, we need to acknowledge our feelings and seek help. Now, I'm not a psychologist I'm a pastor, and this isn't a book on the stages of grief (there are many good ones available), but, it's my opinion that nothing will take the place of our lost loved one, and nothing should.

When we try to fill the void that accompanies death with substitutes such as numbing agents which can lead to addictions, or with people or things that try to take our mind off our loss, we're actually circumventing a very important process in our healing. Grief is natural and necessary. We grieve because we love and we love because we live. Remember, we're not just living our life we're living a part of God's life too, because God is love and God is life. Therefore, God is with us in our love, in our life, and in our death. And yes, He's with us in our grief too. Perhaps now we can begin to see that life and death are in and of themselves healing from God. There is no medicine so healing as uniting ourselves ever more closely to God in this life. And in death, far from being somehow separated from everything, we are united even more closely to God.

So what's the meaning of life? The way I see it there's only one answer that makes any sense at all. The meaning of life is to realize that no matter what happens to us in this world, whether we were raised in a loving and safe home with two loving parents, or if we were left on the streets as an orphan and nothing seemed to go right for us, our life has meaning because we aren't living it in and of ourselves. To live is to participate in the life of God. That's right, all of us are participating in the life of God to varying degrees of awareness. All humanity is created in God's image and the very breath in our bodies is the breath of God. So, in a very real way we're never alone…God is with us, and not just with us, but a part of us.

The Bible teaches us that God is light and in Him there is no darkness.[7] That means no matter how dark things get in our lives, God is always with us. He is present everywhere at all times filling all things. We don't have to feel as if we're walking through a dark life with our hand in front of us stepping carefully so as not to trip and fall. No, we can walk confidently into the rest of our life knowing there is a presence in the darkness that lights our way, and that presence is the uncreated light of the world…Jesus Christ. His presence makes living and dying a holy experience – and that gives us hope.

The idea that each of us is participating in the life of God, in some degree, may be quite a new idea to some of you. Knowing this, I want to unpack it a little more in the next chapter as we consider how it is that just living our lives is actually participating in God's life. So hang in there with me. We're not going to dive off a cliff into the deep waters of thought all alone. What we're doing is kind of like wading out into the deep water; it's a lot easier and safer if someone is holding our hand. I can't promise all of this will make sense to you immediately, but if you hang in there I can promise that God is holding your hand right now, and

---

[7] 1 John 1:5 RSV

I promise you… He won't let go.

A PRESENCE IN THE DARK

"What shall I render to the LORD for all his bounty to me? I will lift up the cup of salvation and call on the name of the LORD,"

Psalm 116:12-13

3

NEVER ALONE

Loneliness is hazardous to our health. Everyone feels alone sometimes. In fact, it's perfectly normal to want to be alone at times. However, it's never normal to feel a chronic sense of loneliness. Studies have shown that a chronic sense of loneliness can increase chances of an early death by 14%[8]

After experiencing the death of a loved one, too often it can be easy to slip into a chronic type of loneliness. It's not even about being physically alone but it feels that way. Experts tell us we don't have to be physically absent from other people to feel alone. We can actually feel alone in a crowd. "Loneliness", says noted psychologist and author Dr. Guy Winch *"... is an entirely subjective state, in which we feel socially and/or*

---

[8] https://www.psychologytoday.com/blog/the-squeaky-wheel/201410/10-surprising-facts-about-loneliness

emotionally disconnected from those around us."[9] Knowing that loneliness is a subjective state is very important; it means we can do something about it.

Just as experts have figured out we can feel alone even when we're not, the great truth of our human existence is we're never really alone because God is with us. As I mentioned in the last chapter, every human being carries within them the breath of God. If that's true, and I believe it is, then why don't we feel God with us? Why are there times, like in the midst of grief, that we feel utterly and completely alone, even though we aren't? The answer to that question will take a little explanation. Please allow me to get a bit theological with you here in order to help us better understand the presence of God in our life.

Humanity was not created by God to just exist, we were created to exist in His presence. The first humans, Adam and Eve, were created to live in His presence in Paradise. There God was always present to them. They were perfect in their relationship to Him and felt nothing of sadness, guilt, or shame. As it was, sin had not yet entered into their world. However, because the only true love is a love that's free, God created them with the freedom to love or not to love, to obey or disobey. When presented with the temptation to disobey what God told them for their own good, they chose to disobey and everything

---

[9] https://www.psychologytoday.com/blog/the-squeaky-wheel/201410/10-surprising-facts-about-loneliness

changed...well, almost everything. You can read all about it in the first few chapters of the Book of Genesis, in the Bible.

After Adam and Eve sinned by choosing to disobey God, they recognized they were no longer in perfect union with Him and death entered into the world. They recognized things had changed. Although they didn't understand the change as death, one thing they did understand was that they no longer felt comfortable in their natural state toward each other. In other words, they realized they were naked and were embarrassed. Things were different, very different. They were even afraid of God's presence so they tried to hide themselves.

But one thing never changed. God never stopped loving Adam and Eve, not one little bit. Why? Because God is eternally good and incapable of changing His feelings, as we humans do. We can't really understand God in His essence. He's too great and beyond our comprehension. However, we can understand His energies of light and love which are at work in our world. He is the source of all light and love. When we love someone, or when they love us, we're actually experiencing a part of God's life in this world. And, as long as we love or feel loved things seem pretty good in life. Why? Because we are experiencing the blessing of God, even though we may not realize it as such.

However, when we experience loss of any kind, including death, things change. We don't feel loved, either because someone left us taking their love with them, or they died and it seems their love is gone. When someone dies, their love seems gone because they're no longer with us physically.

Here we find an important key to understanding life and death…

Because someone is no longer with us physically doesn't mean their love is gone.

Are you still with me? Hang on, this will make more sense as you read a little further. We understand this kind of love when we have to live a long way away from our family. We love them even though we aren't with them and we know they love us. How is that possible? Because God is love and God is life. He transcends time and space so our love is present where they are and their love is present where we are.

Okay, I know this is getting deep theologically so let me try a little pop song philosophy. 90's song artist Phil Collins, probably didn't realize he was singing such great theology when he sang this...

You'll be in my heart. You'll be in my heart. From this day on, now and forever more, you'll be in my heart. You'll be in my heart. No matter what they say, you'll be in my heart, always.[10]

---

[10] "You'll Be In My Heart"; Phil Collins, Walt Disney Records, 1999.

Here is a most important point… **death can't stop love because love is the essence of God.** Love is the greatest force in the world and can't be overcome by anything, not even death. Now, you might be saying *"Sure Brad, of course my love hasn't stopped. I still love him/her."* Of course you do, but what I want you to understand is they still love you too! You're probably thinking "What does that mean?" "They're dead." But, are they really?

Death can't stop life because God is life and all life is eternal because it's flows from His essence. The first thing we must accept if we're to have a better understanding of life is that **life is eternal because it's from God** – and I should add period, full-stop, end of discussion. Life is eternal for all people, of all times, and of all faiths. There's no question that life goes on after death. However, there are many questions as to what life after death is like, and the only answers to that are born by faith; faith in a loving God who is too good to wrong and too wise to make a mistake. You can trust Him.

How can I say that life goes on after physical death? Because, human beings were created for eternity, not just spiritually but physically as well. In order to better understand this, let's look at what Jesus had to say about life, death, and the process of dying.

> *Truly, truly, I say to you, whoever hears my word and believes him who sent me has eternal life. He does not come into judgment, but has passed from death to life.*

> *Truly, truly, I say to you, an hour is coming, and is now here, when the dead will hear the voice of the Son of God, and those who hear will live. For as the Father has life in himself, so he has granted the Son also to have life in himself. And he has given him authority to execute judgment, because he is the Son of Man. Do not marvel at this, for an hour is coming when all who are in the tombs will hear his voice and come out, those who have done good to the resurrection of life, and those who have done evil to the resurrection of judgment.*

-John 5:24-29 ESV

Let's break down Jesus' words into three important points. First, Jesus says whoever believes in the one who sent him into the world (God the Father) **has** eternal life. Now, I love to write, and even though I didn't major in English while in college I know the present tense of a verb when I see one. In any version of the Bible you read these verses, especially in the original Greek, Jesus always says that eternal life is a present possession. That's huge!

Life is eternal because life is from God

Jesus clears up a great misconception for us about death. We don't actually enter eternal life when we die. Instead, we enter eternal life when we believe in God. That's why Jesus clearly states that the believer *"has"* eternal life not *"will have when he dies"*. Eternal life is a present participation in the life and love of God now and forever and unto the ages of ages. Amen! Let that thought soak in for a while. It's mysterious but so is the whole concept of God and eternity.

The second thing we want to understand form this passage is that death is **not** a **permanent** state of being. Death comes to our physical bodies but not to our spirits. We are more than just physical beings (More about that in a moment). Jesus is saying that death is a doorway, something we must all pass through. We don't stay in a state of death.

St. Paul the Apostle speaks of this in his 2nd letter to the Corinthians. In chapter four, speaking to people who'd recently lost loved ones and were concerned about their eternal state he said…

> *But we have this treasure in jars of clay, to show that the surpassing power belongs to God and not to us. We are afflicted in every way, but not crushed; perplexed, but not driven to despair; persecuted, but not forsaken; struck down, but not destroyed;*
>
> - 2 Corinthians 4:7-9 ESV

The body may be destroyed in death, but not life . The true treasure of life is not the body, it's the spirit that lives temporarily in the body, the treasure in the jar of clay. No matter what happens to the body, the treasure (spirit) is not destroyed. That my friends is not only good news, it's reason for hope! The very treasure of our loved one can't be destroyed by death!

The third thing Jesus says that we want to understand from the passage in John 5 is while we live spiritually, even after death, that's not all there is…*we will live again physically as well.* Here is the best news of all. The body of our loved one we lay to rest in death will one day rise again. Jesus calls this the **"...*resurrection of life,*"**

The resurrection of Jesus Christ is the key to everything I'm writing about life and death. Some people choose not to believe in the deity of Jesus Christ because they can't believe in His resurrection from the dead. I'll admit it's a tall order to believe; no one in the history of the world was ever resurrected...till Jesus. However, to believe in the resurrection is not a blind leap of faith. There is more historical, non-biblical support for the life, death, and resurrection of Jesus of Nazareth than for most things we accept as true from our school history books.

C. S. Lewis, the great author and agnostic convert to Christianity said the following about the believability of Jesus as God...

> *I am trying here to prevent anyone saying the really foolish thing that people often say about Him: 'I'm ready to accept Jesus as a great moral teacher, but I don't accept His claim to be God.' That is the one thing we must not say. A man who was merely a man and said the sort of things Jesus said would not be a great moral teacher. He would be either a lunatic — on a level with the man who says he is a poached egg — or else he would be the Devil of Hell. You must make your choice. Either this man was, and is, the Son of God: or else a madman or something worse. You can shut Him up for a fool, you can spit at Him and kill Him as a demon; or you can fall at His feet and call Him Lord and God. But let us not come with any patronising nonsense about His being a great human*

teacher. He has not left that open to us. He did not intend to.[11]

That was pretty straightforward. We all have to deal with who Jesus is. Sadly, many choose not to believe in Jesus because of the many flaws evidenced by many Christians and church leaders over the centuries. However, even if no one ever lived up to the ideals of the Christian faith, it doesn't render them untrue. It simply means everyone is human and humans are always capable of error.

St. Paul the Apostle also had a lot to say about the resurrection of Jesus in his first letter to the Corinthians…

> *Now if Christ is preached as raised from the dead, how can some of you say that there is no resurrection of the dead? But if there is no resurrection of the dead, then Christ has not been raised; if Christ has not been raised, then our preaching is in vain and your faith is in vain. We are even found to be misrepresenting God, because we testified of God that he raised Christ, whom he did not raise if it is true that the dead are not raised. For if the dead are not raised, then Christ has not been raised.* **If Christ has not been raised, your faith is futile and you are still in your sins.** *Then those also who have fallen asleep in Christ have perished. If for this life*

---

[11] Mere Christianity; C.S. Lewis, New York : McMillan Pub. Co., 1952.

only we have hoped in Christ, we are of all men most to be pitied.

But in fact Christ has been raised from the dead, the first fruits of those who have fallen asleep. For as by a man came death, by a man has come also the resurrection of the dead. For as in Adam all die, so also in Christ shall all be made alive. But each in his own order: Christ the first fruits, then at his coming those who belong to Christ. Then comes the end, when he delivers the kingdom to God the Father after destroying every rule and every authority and power. For he must reign until he has put all his enemies under his feet. **The last enemy to be destroyed is death**[12] (Emphasis added)

So, when death comes it's important for us to remember that death isn't the victor, Jesus Christ is. One day death will be no more. Until then, we can find hope in death knowing it's only temporary, and more than that there is another facet of life and death we need to consider; the fellowship we have with those who've died. That may sound crazy to some of you, but stay with me. I'll explain.

The final thought I want to share with you in this chapter is how we realize we're not alone, even after a loved one dies. Let's face it, there is nothing harder than losing a spouse or a child to death. Losing our parents and friends is tough also. All death is tough to deal with, but, when a spouse or child dies it's outside

---

[12] 1 Corinthians 15:12-26 RSV

what we feel is the natural order of things. And, even when we realize life goes on after death, we're left wondering, "What do we about the anxiety that comes from the physical separation? The ancient church's answer to that question was lost to many Western Christians in the fallout from the Protestant Reformation of the sixteenth century; it's imperative that we uncover their answer.

The Early Christians believed in, and taught a doctrine called ***the communion of the saints***. The teaching is part of the confession of the ancient Christian creeds.[13] The belief in a communion between the saints (all Christian believers) living and the saints departed began naturally as a holy tradition. Ancient Christians, like their Jewish Old Testament ancestors, perceived that life went on after death and that those who had gone to the after-life before them, in some way continued in awareness of those left behind. The early Christians began to inscribe words of remembrance on the tombs of the dead. Many of the inscriptions asked the departed to pray for the living who were still on their journey toward Heaven. Such pious thoughts are evidenced by the vision of St John in Revelation 5:8. There we see all the saints of Heaven gathered around the Altar in God's presence with golden bowels full of incense, which he says are "the prayers of the saints".[14]

---

[13] The Nicene Creed, and the Apostle's Creed are the oldest agreed upon confessions of essential Christian belief. The Nicene Creed dates to 325AD.

[14] http://shoebat.com/2014/11/16/powerful-evidence-prove-

Perhaps one of the most beautiful passages of scripture that speaks to the communion we have with those in Heaven is found in the Letter to the Hebrews, chapter 11. The writer recounts the lives of many Old Testament saints who kept the faith, even in the face of great tribulation. Then, in Chapter 12, the writer encourages us who remain in this world to continue on with an enduring faith as we run the race of life *"...surrounded by such a great cloud of witnesses"*.[15] Our loved ones departed are witnesses along with the saints of the ages to the rest of our earthly journey. Your departed loved one is cheering you on. What a comforting and hopeful thought!

So, how does this knowledge that we have a communion or fellowship with our departed loved ones help us in our journey through the feelings of loss and grief? By helping us realize we're never alone. After the death of one as dear as a spouse or child, or perhaps a best friend, we can take comfort in the knowledge that our departed loved one is still with us spiritually, as we are with them. Somehow, in God's great economy their thoughts are still for us. Even though we no longer see them in a physical way, we can sense them in our hearts and spirits thinking of us... praying for us.

Remember St. Paul's words to us earlier about the

---

prayers-saints-part-christianity/;

[15] Hebrews 12:1 RSV

treasure we carry in jars of clay? The real treasure is the spirit of life, not the physical body. The spirit is eternal, but the physical body is temporary. Don't get the wrong idea about the body. Even though temporary the body is to be cherished by us, and rightfully so. After all, this physical body is an integral part of how we know and relate to each other. It's in and through the body that we share the love we have for one another. Here we find yet another promise to bring us hope; **God isn't finished with our mortal bodies – even after we die.**

The body is an integral part of God's greatest creation of the human person. It is too great and too precious to simply be discarded upon our death. That's why God promises us new life in the resurrection of the dead, which is yet to come. We heard this promise earlier as we read the words of Jesus in John 5.

In the next chapter we will explore the beauty and purpose of the body for this world and the next. One thing we can say for sure…no matter where we are or what is happening in life, God isn't through with us yet; and that's true even when we die. There is hope in death!

> "O LORD, I am thy servant;
> I am thy servant, the son of
> thy handmaid. Thou hast
> loosed my bonds."
>
> Psalm 116:16

4

THE BEAUTY OF THE BODY

"Every one of us is, in the cosmic perspective, is precious. If a human disagrees with you, let him live. In a hundred billion galaxies, you will not find another."
Carl Sagan

The highest and most unique thing in all the created world is the human person. I think the quote from Carl Sagan shows how unique we are, and not just in the mind of Christians. Sagan was an avid agnostic, yet he could see the precious nature of humanity. The book of Genesis tells us of this uniqueness. Of all creation, only humans are created in God's image. But what does that mean? Of course, it doesn't mean that we look like God physically. God is spirit yet we know that we too have a spirit which is not only the breath of life, it is the breath of God.

The Hebrew word for spirit is 'ruach'; it's also the word for 'breathe' and it's the word used in the Genesis account of creation...

> ...*then the LORD God formed man of dust from the ground, and* **breathed** *into his nostrils the breath of life; and man became a living being*[16] (Emphasis added)

So, of all the things we can say about what it means to be human, we can say that it means we have a body and a spirit. But that's not all, even an animal has a body and spirit, and we're definitely more than an animal (although we humans sometimes act like one).

The one thing that is unique to humans and makes us the highest created thing is a third component that accompanies body and spirit – the mind. The mind is that part of our human existence that completes our being made in the image of God. It is what gives us the power of intellect and reason, and it's what separates us from the animal world. Body, mind, and spirit show us to be of Trinitarian form, which is another aspect of our being made in the image of God, Whom in His essence is three persons, Father, Son, and Holy Spirit, one in essence and undivided.

While, this isn't a book about theology I do want to say a few words to speak to this greatest of all mysteries, the Holy Trinity. How God's being can be Trinitarian and undivided is a complete mystery, yet

---

[16] Genesis 2:7 RSV

the early Christians understood God as such. Even in the Old Testament God often spoke of himself in the plural, such as in Genesis 1:26 where He said *"Let **US** make man in **Our** image, after **OUR** likeness"* (emphasis added).

From of old, many have struggled to understand this Trinitarian mystery, some even rejecting it while still holding to a belief in one God. Here is a critical point we must recognize if we are to come to grips with life and find hope in death; to understand God is impossible. God is incomprehensible by definition… and so are life and death. Ultimately, our life and our death must be embraced as a mystery. **Only in eternity will we understand our existence and all that happened in and through us in this world.** Until then, we must embrace the mystery by faith; faith in God for this life… and for the next.

Forgive me for digressing into such deep theology for a moment. These things needed to be said if we're to grasp what the body is all about. Each of the three components of our humanity, body, mind, and spirit are sacred. However, it's through the body that we experience much of what it means to be alive.

In the fullness of humanity there are five senses: hearing, touching, seeing, smelling and tasting. However, while one or more of these senses may not be present at birth, or can be lost over time, the sense of touch is critical to our realizing we're alive. Now, I'm not a doctor or scientist, but I think I can say that touching and the realization we gain by touching is critical to living. Human beings can be deaf, unable to speak, blinded, robbed of the sense of smell and taste, and still think and function to some extent in society. but if we're unable to feel the sense of touch somewhere in our body, then we would be in what doctors call a persistent vegetative state.

I don't want us to get bogged down in some technical medical discussion. However, I do want to point out that I believe even a person in a vegetative state is still a living being as long as they have the breath of God in them. However, the sense of touch is integral to the human experience.

Living beings desire the sense of touch; this is true of more than just humans. Every day when I rise and when I come home from work, our two dogs, Buddy and Gibby, can't wait for me to acknowledge them by patting their heads. In fact, my speaking to them isn't enough. They will follow me around the house until I stop and pet them. Touching is a vital way of communicating in life.

It's fascinating to me how Michelangelo chose to communicate the importance of the sense of touch in his famous fresco, the *'Creation of Man'* in the Sistine Chapel. He shows the finger of God reaching out and nearly touching the tip of Adam's finger. Or is it Adam reaching out to touch God's finger? Oh well, I'll leave that one for smarter people than me. The desire for touch is an innate response in humanity, and not only in humanity, but I think it's safe to say that God desires to touch us as well.

While God touched humanity with His breath of life, that alone didn't keep humans in their perfectly created state of being. As we discussed in chapter two, in the sin of our first ancestors all humanity became separated from God. But God loved His most prized creation so much that He desired to touch us once again in a way that would reconcile us to Him forever. In a way that would heal us for time and eternity. He touched all of humanity by becoming truly human.

In the greatest, most mystical act of God that we are invited to meditate on – God became human. I know, it boggles my mind too, but that is exactly what happened in the **Incarnation** of Jesus Christ. Incarnation is a big theological term for God taking human flesh upon himself (more on the meaning of incarnation in Chapter 5). Jesus Christ, the second person of the Holy Trinity, God's only begotten son, became man. Why? Because the human person and the human body were created by God to be sacred. By taking on human flesh Jesus sanctified the matter of creation. In other words, He made matter, matter.

All of creation is sacred because it exists by God's word and power. However, when we humans lost our original beauty and holiness through sin, death came into existence as a consequence. God loved us too much to let us die an eternal death. He sent his son Jesus into the world that through His perfect life, death, and resurrection, we would not die forever, but be reconciled to Him in eternal life.

Our reconciliation to God through Jesus Christ has many stages, but three are of specific importance to this discussion. *First*, is when we believe. By faith in Christ, we become aware that God is with us. He hasn't left us alone and without a savior. *Secondly*, we are reconciled to Him even more fully in our death. St. Paul testifies that to die is to be with Christ.[17] *Thirdly*, we are fully reconciled to Him for all eternity in the resurrection of our bodies at the end of the age.

To say we don't die forever implies that we do die temporarily. When our bodies experience physical death we must remember the words of Jesus we read in chapter three; death isn't a permanent state of being, rather, it's a doorway we all must pass through. In death our bodies cease to hold the breath of God that gives life to all living things. However, the spirit and mind are not dependent upon God's breath. We continue to live in spirit as we surrender our spirit and mind back to God who gave them to us.

So what are we to understand about the body in death? It is the sacred vessel of God's choosing for housing our spirit and mind while in the physical world. Furthermore, it's sacred not just because it houses our spirit and mind, but because it houses God's Spirit as well. Our spirit only lives because of God's Spirit. St. Paul the Apostle tells us that our bodies are temples of

---

[17] 2 Corinthians 5:8 RSV

the Living God because His Spirit abides in us.[18] Remember, God is life and life is God.

Therefore, how we treat our bodies matters not only in life, but also in death. Christian burial rites show this to be the case. We carefully and reverently lay the bodies of our loved ones to rest, in the hope of their rising again. The earliest Christians anticipated the coming resurrection of our mortal bodies to be reunited with our spirits at the end of time. Listen carefully to the words of St. Paul as he describes this hope using the metaphor of sleep for physical death:

> *For since we believe that Jesus died and rose again, even so, through Jesus, God will bring with him those who have fallen asleep. For this we declare to you by the word of the Lord, that we who are alive, who are left until the coming of the Lord, shall not precede those who have fallen asleep. For the Lord himself will descend from heaven with a cry of command, with the archangel's call, and with the sound of the trumpet of God. And the dead in Christ will rise first; then we who are alive, who are left, shall be caught up together with them in the clouds to meet the Lord in the air; and so we shall always be with the Lord. Therefore comfort one another with these words.*
> -1 Thessalonians 4:14-18

If our bodies are so precious to God that He refuses to cast them away into oblivion upon our death, but will raise them up again in His good time, then

---

[18] 1 Corinthians 6:19 RSV

shouldn't it matter to us how we treat them? The only answer that makes sense is a resounding YES! The human body is the most beautiful of all created things, a work of art unparalleled anywhere in the universe. All human bodies are unique; they are an intricate part of who we are.

One of the first heresies (wrong teachings) the early Christians had to deal with was the teaching by some that the body was unimportant in the grand scheme of life. The heresies taught that only the soul and spirit were what mattered. This thinking crept into several schools of thought. *Gnostics*, who took their name from the Greek word for knowledge *'Gnosis,'* actually taught that it didn't matter what we did with the body. God only resided in the spirit world, they said, completely missing the point of the Incarnation of God in Jesus Christ. This critical flaw led to the teaching that physical things were evil and could therefore be discarded or mistreated. As a result, sexual morality wasn't important to many Gnostics. They felt what was done with the body was of no concern to God.

We can see such Gnostic thinking is still present today in our culture's rapidly declining sense of morality. Immorality has been around since the first sins of our ancestors. However, our Western culture is presently devaluing almost every teaching of scripture on the uniqueness of our creation as male and female at an alarming rate. On our present course of understanding, there will soon be whole generations born into a world that don't recognize any value to our importance and uniqueness as male and female. What we believe about the human body is very important.

Another heretical teaching was that of *'Docetism,'* from the Greek word for "seem" or "illusion". Docetism taught that Jesus' physical body was only an apparition and that He was never really human. Again the danger of such thinking is that it devalues the human body. If indeed God took on human form, as Christianity teaches in the Incarnation, then the body is holy and of infinite value.

Such heretical beliefs as Gnosticism and Docetism have never fully gone away. They continue to resurface, to varying degrees, in every generation as human beings grapple with the meaning of life and death. Where we see cultures devaluing respect for humanity there is usually an undercurrent of such heresies, though often subconscious. Such trends should give us cause to stop and evaluate how and what we think of human life.

When we understand the proper place and role of our human body in the world, we honor God and each other. We recognize that there is something of the Divine in every person, and such knowledge leads us to a proper love for the human body, a love that builds up and accepts, not one that tears down and rejects. By perceiving in the human body the beauty intended by God, we also begin to see everyone as His child regardless of race, creed, color, or any other persuasion that's different from ours. There is a solidarity to the human race that transcends our differences.

Chances are pretty good that those of you reading this book have felt the pain of those heretical divisions. How do we get the proper message of beauty and solidarity out there into a world fractured by division and false teaching? The best way I know is to get involved in the incarnational work of Jesus Christ in the world. Do you remember what the word incarnation means? It means to take on flesh. So how do we *'take on flesh'* for the work of Jesus Christ in the world? **We learn to serve others out of their needs not our wants.** Allow me to tell you the story of how I learned the meaning of living *incarnational* for others in the next chapter.

A PRESENCE IN THE DARK

> "I will offer to thee the sacrifice of thanksgiving and call on the name of the LORD. I will pay my vows to the LORD in the presence of all his people,"
>
> Psalm 116:17-18

5

INCARNATIONAL LIVING

In my work as a Christian minister I've done literally hundreds of funerals over the last ten years, not because that many people died in my church, thank the Lord ... but, because of my association with Broadway Mortuary in Wichita, KS. Cozine Memorial Group, which owns Broadway Mortuary, offers a wide variety of funeral service, cremation and cemetery options.

Unlike many funeral firms I've worked with, the Cozine family and their employees live out their commitment to the families they serve with an unparalleled professionalism and sense of care. The Cozine family has owned and operated the Broadway Mortuary for three generations.

Many years ago, one of the owners, Mr. Ashley Cozine, took note of the work I did in helping a family from my church plan and hold a funeral service at the Mortuary chapel. When a future need arose with a family the mortuary was working with who didn't have a church home to help them navigate the troubling waters of their grief, I was recommended to help them plan... I was honored to help.

All of my prior funeral experiences had been with church families who were under my pastoral care, but this opportunity was different. I didn't know the family in need or their loved one who'd died, and they didn't know me. In the experience of trying to bring comfort to strangers suffering in sorrow, God showed me something I think is incredibly important – **no one is a stranger to God.** He also showed me that if I was truly His servant, they weren't strangers to me either. They were my brothers and sisters in humanity, regardless of their faith, or lack thereof.

More opportunities began to come my way as my friends at Broadway Mortuary began to call on me to do more and more services for families with either no church home, or no spiritual guide to help them. I've learned many things through those experiences. While many of the people I've helped had a nominal belief in God, but hadn't stayed with any church, others have had no spiritual background at all.

I've had opportunities to help families with just about every background imaginable. I've done services for people who self-identified as Catholic yet didn't belong to a parish and thus had no priest to help them. A few of the services I've done have even been for atheists. You might wonder how a Christian minister can speak words of comfort over someone who had no belief in

God. So did I. But God showed me his love for them was not conditioned upon whether they loved Him back. Likewise, He showed me my love and service to them was not conditioned upon their belief, or lack thereof. Rather, my service to them was to be offered because they were my brothers and sisters in humanity, and as such deserved the dignity of a proper burial, as well as my prayers for their eternal peace in the hands of their maker.

Sometimes, families find themselves in difficult situations making funeral service plans. The burial customs of a particular church the family self-identifies with don't always match up with the beliefs they've come to hold. This happened to a Catholic family I helped. Their parish priest said he couldn't do the service since the cremated ashes were not going to be interred. The family wanted to take the ashes home. Apparently that conflicted with Catholic teaching. However, the family still needed the comfort of a Christian burial.

Having a Catholic background from my youth I empathized with their need. They were devastated in the midst of their grief, having to choose between the teaching of the church and their own personal desire to keep their loved one's ashes. I'm not passing judgment on the Catholic teaching. When explained properly they have some very valid points that support their teaching. However, God always makes a way to meet the grieving needs of His children. The Lord told me to put on my clergy collar (something very few Protestants do today), and give them a service with a

Catholic feel and with Catholic prayers (which I already knew) in an effort to meet their need. After that experience, I think my friends at Broadway Mortuary realized they could ask me to help anyone.

One of the most interesting services I held was for an Eastern Orthodox family. The father who died hadn't been particularly faithful to the church, and his kids hadn't either. However when the father died, because the kids wanted to have the father cremated, the church refused the service based on their teaching against cremation. Again, I'm not passing judgment on the Orthodox teaching. In fact, I find their reasons quite compelling as they are born out of love and devotion to the sacredness of the human body. Still something had to be done to help a grieving family to see that God loved them and that He cared about the loss of their father.

So, once again I put on my clergy collar, learned a few Orthodox prayers and customs, and held a graveside service as best I could. I've had several more occasions of a similar nature since then. In all of them, God has taught me to get outside of my own denominational culture and serve in an *incarnational* way.

Incarnational living, Wow! That's a mouthful. It sure sounds good but what does it mean? At its simplest level it means doing things for others in tangible ways they can relate to, even if you don't want to. However, there's a deeper understanding that will help us embrace the dark mystery that shrouds us when death enters into our lives.

Incarnational living demands that we get out of our comfort zone and be what others need us to be, whether we want to or not.

In the gospel of John 1:14 we read this about the Incarnation of Jesus *"The Word became flesh and made his dwelling among us."* Why did God choose to make His dwelling among us? The simple answer is to save us from our sins. The perfect life, death, and resurrection of Jesus Christ made atonement for the sins of humanity. As true as that is there is still something more to it, and many people miss out completely on what that something more is. God sent His only son into the world because he loved us. He loved us too much to leave us estranged from Himself and from each other. Everything God does is ultimately motivated by His love for His creation.

Incarnational living demands that we get out of our comfort zone and be what others need us to be – whether we want to or not. Why? Because Jesus did it for us and He calls us to do it for each other. Jesus took this whole incarnational thing to the extreme by dying for us. It was the only way to reconcile us to God, so He did. And, truth be told incarnational living is the only way to truly show our love for others, because in doing so we show we love them for who they are.

When our loved ones die, those left behind can become so shrouded in darkness they can't find the light of life on their own. They really need a friend to come near and be present. Your presence with a grieving friend isn't about having answers to ease the pain. There aren't any. In fact, we make it worse when we try to say things like, *"It's okay. I know it hurts but you'll get over it."* No. It isn't okay. Death hurts like nothing else in the world and we are never the same again.

In the back of this book you will find an open letter from my friend and colleague, Billy Byler. Two months before Billy and his wife Shelley's second wedding anniversary, she died of liver cancer. She was only 24 years old. Billy was now a 25 year old widower; thankfully something with which very few people can identify. For Billy, life was never going to be the same again. However, the incarnational living of people in his church made all the difference. They were there for him, not with answers – there weren't any, but with their presence.

What a grieving friend needs is our presence and our love. They need to know we care, that we grieve with them. That's what God does. That's right…God grieves with us. You might think that God grieving with us is a strange thought. But if God is love, then God cares, because to love is to care. And if we care, we hurt. God knows our grief and He wants us to know one others' as well.

So, the greatest thing we can do for those who are grieving the loss of a loved one is to do what Jesus did – enter in to their pain. We must show our love for them in incarnational ways. When Jesus took on flesh to born a human child, He too entered into the pain of living in a fallen world. All the pains of life that we endure, He endured as well.

The Bible doesn't record all the pains Jesus felt. Like when one of his uncles or aunts died or perhaps his grandparents. He chose to be born an infant and to grow up in this world just like we do so that we could know our God feels our pain. Even if it seems no one else on earth understands the pain and agony we experience in this life – Jesus does.

That's why the ministry of our presence to those who've lost loved ones is so important. When we comfort the bereaved, we are the comfort of God to them. St. Paul said it like this:

> *Praise be to the God and Father of our Lord Jesus Christ, the Father of compassion and the God of all comfort, who comforts us in all our troubles, so that we can comfort those in any trouble with the comfort we ourselves receive from God.*
>
> -2 Corinthians 1:3-4 NIV

Paul goes on to say that we can learn something from our own pain and suffering…

> *For just as we share abundantly in the sufferings of Christ, so also our comfort abounds through Christ. If we are distressed, it is for your comfort and salvation; if we are comforted, it is for your comfort, which produces in you patient endurance of the same sufferings we suffer. And our hope for you is firm, because we know that just as you share in our sufferings, so also you share in our comfort.*

-2 Corinthians 1:5-7 NIV

When we suffer we're actually sharing in Christ's suffering. But if we share in His suffering, we also share in His comfort. And we must remember, He is the God of **ALL** comfort.

Incarnational living is sharing in the pain and suffering of others, just like Jesus did ours.

What good news. When we share in the sufferings of others we're bringing God's comfort, and there's no better comfort than that.

In all the funerals I've ever officiated, I've never seen one that wasn't attended by at least a few friends of the deceased or family. I'm sure somewhere there's been a funeral service held where no one showed up to help the family mourn their loss. What a sad thought. However, even if that's true, the family wasn't alone. There was a presence there in the midst of their darkness and that presence was God. He always shows up.

Furthermore, even if we don't realize God is with us in our grief, we're still blessed to mourn our loss in what feels all alone. In His sermon on the Mount, Jesus pronounced words of blessings for those who live according to certain truths. One of those truthful blessings was to announce that everyone who mourns is blessed because they too will be comforted.

Blessed are those who mourn, for they shall be comforted.[19]

To mourn our loss is to feel deeply the pain of the void we experience when someone we love dies. Jesus speaks of this mourning as something positive in our lives. Anything that brings a blessing to us is ultimately a good thing for our lives. But how are we blessed by mourning?

It does seem hard to understand how mourning over death can bring us a blessing. For the most part, we don't feel the blessing right away. I think the best way to try and understand this is not to think of a cause and effect relationship between mourning and blessings. Just because we mourn doesn't mean that we will be blessed right away. Blessings always come in God's sovereign time.

So, what can we say about this unusual blessing? We can say that God has promised to not let our mourning go unnoticed. And even if we feel all alone in our grief, God is with us. He will not leave us without comfort. And when we realize the comfort of our friends and family is really the comfort of God, then we've realized our true blessing.

Having friends and family around us when we're grieving is a tremendous blessing, but having the comfort of God is even greater. If you're experiencing

---

[19] Matthew 5:4 RSV

the fresh grief of a lost loved one as you read this book, you know what I mean. Where would we be without that friend who literally took over when we didn't have the presence of mind to make all the decisions that had to be made when death came? Or, what about that brother or sister who stepped in to raise a younger brother or sister when their parents died prematurely? There are a myriad of other scenarios. All of them are examples of incarnational living. We need them. We can't live without them. They all come to us because two thousand years ago God sent His son into the world to become flesh and blood, to take on pain and sorrow, and most importantly of all – to conquer death forever. Because Christ came and conquered the grave, you and I can choose to live forever through Him, even though we die!

Jesus said to her, "I am the resurrection and the life; he who believes in me, though he die, yet shall he live, and whoever lives and believes in me shall never die. Do you believe this?
-John 11:25-26

Those words are amazing! How is it that we never die? Death is so real. Our departed loved ones aren't with us anymore. What could be more real than that? Even so, Jesus invites us into the mystery of life and death. Death is but a doorway we all must pass through; it's not a permanent state of being. What we see looks permanent yet with eyes of faith we can see that our departed loved ones are still very much alive.

The incarnation of Jesus Christ is the greatest gift ever

given, and because of it we receive peace, love, and joy for this world, and eternal life for the next. Scripture tells us every good and prefect gift is from God, the Father of lights[20]. The incarnational living we experience from others in this world are actually God's gifts to us as He sheds His light on our sometimes dark and lonely paths.

As you finish this chapter, stop and think about the incarnational gifts God has given you. why don't you do a little exercise. Make a list right now of the people who have made a difference in your life in an incarnational way, who helped you through difficult times. Why not make your list right here in this book. I think you'll find it healing to reflect upon all the ways God has blessed you, even in the midst of your grief. He really does care. Knowing others care helps us to know God cares, and that gives us hope that as St. Paul says in Romans 5, *"...hope does not disappoint"*.[21]

---

[20] James 1:17 RSV

[21] Romans 5:5 NAS

MY INCARNATIONAL LIST

Name of Person - Help Given/Acknowledged

A PRESENCE IN THE DARK

> *"Precious in the sight of the LORD is the death of his saints."*

Psalm 116:15

6

REMOVING THE SHROUD

Death has always been shrouded in mystery. Try to imagine if you can, how the first persons who ever experienced the death of a loved one must have felt. The Bible tells us Adam and Eve were the first to feel this way. The death they experienced was one of the worst possible. Their son Cain, killed their other son, Abel. Murder within a family; it's hard to imagine worse. If your life's been touched by a similar heinous act of violence my heart and prayers reach out to you. Death comes in a variety of ways, but murder has to be the hardest to cope with.

No one is ever prepared for such a violent act. Adam and Eve had nothing with which to compare their new found feelings brought on by the death of their son. There was no church they could go to for comfort. There was no such thing as professional counseling. No one had ever died before let alone been murdered. Yet with such grim circumstances they weren't completely helpless. They still had God. And as we learned in the last chapter, God's comfort is the best of all.

Adam and Eve knew life was different after their fall from grace. Once sin entered their lives they had new feelings to deal with – grief and guilt. What were these strange new feelings? How could they deal with them? The good news was they still had a relationship with God, not as direct as it was in paradise, but He was still guiding them through life with all its new twists and turns.

It's important for us to take some time and talk about how to deal with guilt. It's one of the major factors in determining how we feel about ourselves and our interactions with others. If we don't learn how to understand guilt and the way it affects us, then the meaning of life, both ours and our departed loved ones, will be shrouded with doubt. We won't be able to see the true meaning of things until the shroud of guilt is removed.

In order to begin to remove the shroud of uncertain feelings brought on by death, we must recognize the types of guilt and be willing to acknowledge our grief. There are two types of guilt, true and false. And believe it or not they're not always easy to tell apart. True guilt is what it sounds like. There's something we've done for which our conscience accuses us. We're guilty. We did wrong and we know it. We need help dealing with the remorse of such knowledge.

False guilt however, is not nearly as easy to discern.

There isn't a clear picture of what we've done wrong, yet we still feel guilty. Such feelings of guilt complicate our grief and stall our healing. But why do we feel the guilt? When it comes to the death of our loved ones, the guilt we feel is usually because we're trying to explain something that can't be explained.

Some deaths can be explained by actions, of course. Like when someone lived a life of physical abuse and neglect and it hastened their death. In such cases, while their death is explainable, there wasn't anything anyone could've done to prevent it if the person wasn't willing to help him or herself. Cases of abuse and addiction are difficult from many perspectives but one thing is for certain… we can't make another person change his or her behavior, no matter how hard we try.

As you might have guessed, much of what plagues us in our daily lives is false guilt. False guilt often stems from our feeling that if we'd done something differently, then the outcome would somehow be different. But that's not always true. With false guilt our mind accuses us of doing something wrong when we didn't, or that we didn't do something we should have. We're then led to the wrongful conclusion that things could have been different if we hadn't made such mistakes.

These feelings of false guilt trap us into a vicious cycle of trying to figure out what we did wrong. We play the scenarios over and over in our mind trying to determine the cause of our feelings of guilt. If we are going to put an end to this vicious cycle we must call it for what it is – a lie.

False guilt is an ugly lie. However, when false guilt attacks us in the wake of death it's particularly destructive; it circumvents the natural grieving process. We mistakenly feel we could have changed the outcome of our loved one's death. I've seen mothers tragically go over and over their every action trying to figure out what they did wrong when their infant died for no apparent reason. I've also seen parents blame themselves for the death of their child who died in an auto accident by thinking their child would still be alive if only they'd stopped them from going wherever they were when the accident occurred.

False guilt is especially destructive when death results from suicide. While there are many tragic forms of death, suicide may be the most. When a loved one takes their own life, there simply is no explanation that will satisfy our nagging question of why. We are left with very complicated feelings of wanting to blame someone. In a murder we have someone to blame. But in suicide who do we blame? Many times we blame ourselves, thinking we could've somehow stopped this tragedy.

It's been my experience that such feelings of thinking we could've prevented the suicide usually stem from false guilt. Over the years, two of my work associates committed suicide. I watched the pain and agony of the families left behind. Jeff was a 21 year-old male model with an addiction to drugs. No one would have ever imagined that he had such inner struggles. Bill, was a middle aged married man who was also a hypochondriac and continually needed reassurance of love. Both were not just my co-workers, they were my friends. I couldn't believe the news of their suicide when I received it.

Both families were obviously devastated. However, Jeff's parents had strong a Christian faith and displayed an amazing strength. Although I'm sure they had some initial wondering of what, if anything, they could have done differently to prevent Jeff's tragedy. Bill and his wife were nominal believers at best. Several times I listened to her blame herself. She was riddled with false guilt. She wasn't to blame. Bill had serious emotional issues that he often hid very well. Bill's wife's guilt was a false one. False guilt is a lie and a vicious cycle that must be stopped.

If any of this is starting to feel familiar to you, please hear what I'm about to say. I want to say to you with all my heart…**the death of your loved one is NOT your fault!** There is nothing you could have done to prevent their death. There are many times when death just doesn't make sense, but then again – neither does life.

There's only one way to make sense of life and death. We must learn to see our place in the larger story of the world. If you believe in God, it matters who your God is. Many people believe in a God of their own making or one that was imposed on them by the community in which they grew up. It's been my experience after almost 20 years of Pastoral ministry that many people have an extremely flawed image of who God really is. Let's face it, it's difficult to see who God really is when so much of what we base Him on are projections of our own human flaws.

We must learn to open our hearts to a new understanding of God and to the incarnational acts of love shown us by others. Each time we experience the unconditional love of someone we're actually experiencing the truth of who God is. He is so much more than just a deity in which to believe. God is a divine and perfect life in which we are invited to participate.

One of the first things we must accept if we are to participate in the life of God is that grief is natural. As humans, God designed us with the capacity to grieve, which is in actuality to have a profound sense of our loss. It's important for us to know that God understands our grief. He understands our grief through the human life of Jesus Christ. As man, Jesus grieved the loss of his own friends and loved ones. The Bible tells us that Jesus wept at the loss of His dear friend Lazarus. We also learn about God experiencing grief when St. Paul warns that by our sinful actions we *"…grieve the Holy Spirit…"*[22]

We must be careful not to apply too much literalism to the thought of God grieving. Grief is a human emotion and God is not human, except in the life of

---

[22] Ephesians 4:30 RSV

His son Jesus. In reality, God transcends all that is human by his divine nature yet He describes himself in scripture in human terms so we can better relate to him and know He cares.

> *Are not two sparrows sold for a penny? And not one of them will fall to the ground without your Father's will. But even the hairs of your head are all numbered. Fear not, therefore; you are of more value than many sparrows.*
> -Matthew 10:29-31

In order to embrace life and death as we should we must learn to know the true God. That sounds trite. I don't mean it as such. God wants us to know him. In fact, all of history is the story of His calling out to humanity to win us back into communion with Him. Everything is ready. Through Jesus Christ we can enter again into communion with our Maker. Paradise was lost in the sin of Adam and Eve, but is now being restored through Christ. It won't be fully restored until Christ comes again to usher in the new and perfect age, but we're well on the way.

Another thing we must accept if we're to realize our participation in the life of God is that He really does care what happens to us. As you get to know the true God you will have to let go of old stereotypes, your false narratives about God. Sadly, many people have been taught that God is some distant deity who put the world in motion and then left us alone. Another version is that God doesn't leave us alone all of the time; sometimes he openly punishes us for our mistakes, or other times arbitrarily withholds His blessings to "teach us a lesson." But all of these are not who God is; they are who humanity has made him out to be.

So, how do we get to know the real God? I know I've said before this isn't a book about theology, but it's critical that we begin at the right place. I'm going to give you three steps to set you out on the right path to knowing the real God. "Just three," you ask? Yep, just three. Everything builds on these three truths.

1. Forget everything you've been taught; it's probably wrong, unless it's one of the following two points.

2. Begin by accepting that God is, in His essence, nothing but love – pure, holy, unconditional love.

3. Understand that everything God does is motivated by His love... yes, even His judgements.

When we come to a place of understanding these things about God, we're ready to learn. We will now have a platform of truth from which to discover new things about Him as He reveals Himself to us through life...and death.

The greatest shroud of mystery surrounding death stems from a wrong understanding of who God is. He doesn't want us to die, He never did. But, He loved us too much to make us like robots without any self-will. Instead God made us perfectly free. Free to love or free to hate. There was no other way because real love, pure, holy, unconditional love only operates in freedom. We can't force someone to love us, and neither can God.

It's always a little uneasy when I speak about God in a *'can't do'* kind of way. You know, like God can't do this or God can't do that. We don't like saying God can't do anything, because most of us have been taught that God CAN do anything He wants. He's God! But, there's one thing God can't do – He can't violate His own nature which is pure love. If He could, then He wouldn't be God.

Once we remove the shroud of false understanding about God and His nature we're free to see life and death in a completely different way. We're free to see the hope that fills all of life no matter how dark things get. And, we're free to see the hope that exists in death. In the next chapter I want to explore the concept of finding hope in death; it truly is a paradigm shift in how we must think.

Hang in there with me. I know we've talked about some really deep theological thoughts along the way, but we're almost home. I can hear singer John Legend encouraging you now…

> *And maybe the world ain't what it could be*
> *But to understand why is to know reality*
> *Ah don't give in (hang on in there)*

Ah I said hang on (hang on in there)[23]

---

[23] "Hang On in There"; Mike James Kirkland, John Legend and The Roots, G.O.O.D. and Columbia Records. 2010

A PRESENCE IN THE DARK

> "I love the LORD, because he has heard my voice and my supplications.
> Because he inclined his ear to me, therefore I will call on him as long as I live."

Psalm 116:1-2

7

FINDING HOPE

Hope springs eternal in the human breast;
Man never is, but always to be blest.
The soul, uneasy and confin'd from home,
Rests and expatiates in a life to come.
Alexander Pope

The concept of hope for a better life in a better world is pretty much a universal thought throughout every age and culture. 18th Century writer, Alexander Pope's words seem to capture our unresolved longing because they speak to the heart of our human condition. There is a sense in which we never quite feel blessed in this life, but in reality we are. Pope speaks to not feeling quite at home in this life, in this world.

Where is home? I was born in Kansas so I guess I could say that's my home. But, I also lived in Texas and it felt like home while I was there. There's an old saying I'm sure you've heard, *"Home is where the heart is."*

I've always tried to live by that moto. Later, I moved back to Kansas and people said "Well, you're going home, Aren't you?" But the truth was, I made Texas my home. I remember a bumper sticker that I really liked; it said **"I wasn't born in Texas, but I got here as soon as I could."** As a pastor, I gave my heart to the people in San Antonio so it was hard to pack up and move, even back to a place with which I was familiar.

But, are we ever really at home anywhere? Some people grow up moving from state to state and never seem to settle down. Others stay in one town, even one house their entire lives. But was that their home? Isn't the very thought of home to be somewhere permanent? The first definition of the word 'Home', according to the Bing internet search dictionary says it's *"the place where one lives permanently, especially as a member of a family or household."* When we die, as we all will someday, the place we've called home, whether for long or short, will cease to be our home.

In reality we're all Pilgrims on a journey. We're on a journey to a place of permanence, and this earthly life is definitely not permanent. There's an old gospel song written by Albert E. Brumley that speaks to this reality…

> *This world is not my home, I'm just passing through*
> *My treasures are laid up somewhere beyond the blue*
> *The angels beckon me from Heaven's open door*

And I can't feel at home in this world anymore. [24]

So, if this world isn't my home then where is? To answer that question I need to tell you a little more about my personal journey through life. Remember, each of us is on a Pilgrim's journey; we're all travelling from somewhere to somewhere else.

When I was a young man in my twenties I loved to sing in the church choir. I even sang in some men's ensemble's and quartets. One of the songs we sang was the one I just quoted "This World Is Not My Home." I remember thinking how profound that was. At 22 years of age I hadn't really thought much about the fact that I was a transient in this world. I doubt many do at that age.

The song was fun but it didn't move me to some significant realization that I was going to die someday, nor that I shouldn't get too attached to this world and all that's in it, which is precisely what we do in life. We get very attached to the things and people of this world, which in and of itself isn't a bad or abnormal thing.

As I aged and got married and had kids, I slowly began to realize just how temporary my life was in this world. Once my wife and I had kids time seemed to fly by! I spent the first 21 years of my life in a hurry to grow up; it seemed like a very long time. But once my wife

---

[24] "This World is Not My Home"; Albert E. Brumley, 1937

and I had our two kids, the next two decades went by in what seemed like a blink of an eye. Really, it just doesn't feel like 22 years since our first child was born.

However, there were a couple of events in life that grabbed my attention about how fast I was moving toward eternity. One was when I began to teach our son Corbin how to drive. When he got his license and headed off to the first day of school driving himself, all of a sudden I couldn't believe where the time had gone. And our daughter was just 2 years behind him!

The second thing was more gradual but still had a powerful effect on my sense of time and eternity. One day I realized that as a minister, I was now doing more funerals than weddings – way more. We were all aging. And all of a sudden we seemed to be aging faster and faster. Years went by in what seemed only a few months.

Of course time doesn't change; it goes by at the same pace. However, our perspective of time changes radically as we age. This changing perspective can often leave people feeling unfulfilled, even depressed. We feel like we don't have as much time as we used to in order to accomplish all our life goals. Although, in reality we never had a guarantee of any amount of time in which to live in this world.

The real challenge of this change in perspective is to not let it steal your joy, your hope for living. I'm 56 as I write this book. If I live to be 90 I still have 34 years left. From the time I was born until our first child was born was exactly 34 years. As I look back on it all, those first 34 years seem like a lot of time. When I think about it like that it gives me hope. Hope is always a matter of perspective.

So, what's the answer to living in this world with hope and purpose? Volumes could be written, and have, about how to live with purpose in life, but that's not really the scope of this book. However, I will say that when we come to a place that we can accept our transient nature in this world, it becomes easier to see our real purpose in this life.

Our real purpose in life is to love – love God and love each other. If we live with love in our hearts, we've fulfilled the purpose of our human existence. But how to live with hope in this life is a bit harder to answer. Hope is critical to human existence. So many things rob us of our hope, if we let them.

So far, I've invited you to consider several things about how we should understand life and death. Things like: what life is all about, how loneliness is hazardous to our health, that we're never really alone, the beauty of the physical body and how we should relate to it, the benefits of living incarnational lives, and I've tried to help remove the shroud of mystery that surrounds life and death.

Now, in this final chapter I want to help you find hope, real hope – even in the face of death. To do so, we must begin with trying to understand just what is hope. I think the best definition of Hope I've ever heard is that it's *a feeling of desire and trust; desire for something essential to happen, and trust that it will.*

Listen to what famed motivational speaker and author, the late Dr. Wayne Dyer said about hope…

> *What is hope but a feeling of optimism, a thought that says things will improve, it won't always be bleak,* **there's a way to rise above the present circumstances.** *Hope is an internal awareness that you do not have to suffer forever, and that somehow, somewhere there is a remedy for despair that you will come upon if you can only maintain this expectancy in your heart.*[25] (Emphasis added)

While Dr. Dyer wasn't necessarily writing from a Christian perspective, he was right on when he said *"…there's a way to rise above the present circumstances."* I hope you'll take a moment to really listen to what I'm about to say. No matter how dark your present situation feels, no matter how deep of grief you feel, you haven't fallen farther than God can reach, and He's reaching out to you – **right now!**

The darkness that seems to envelope us when death comes to our loved ones isn't real, it's an illusion. The pain and loss are definitely real, but the darkness isn't. Let me explain how darkness isn't real in our life.

It's a scientific fact that dark and light can't co-exist together. Darkness is the absence of light. But

---

[25] http://www.notable-quotes.com/h/hope_quotes_iv.html

introduce even the smallest little ray of light and everything changes. For instance, if you're in a perfectly dark room where you can't see anything, not even your hand in front of your face, then introduce even a tiny ray of light and your eyes will eventually adjust to the darkness around you. Why? Because light always dispels dark. In every battle between dark and light, light wins. It's a fact of science.

Right now you may be thinking, *"Sure Brad, that makes sense from a scientific point of view, but it doesn't change the fact that I feel darkness all around me in my grief, and knowing science doesn't change how I feel."* True. But, I know something that will. Well, not something but someone.

St. John's gospel tells us that Jesus Christ is the light of the world, and that His light is continually coming to us such that darkness has not overcome it.[26] Light is one of John's favorite metaphors for Jesus. In his first Epistle, John tells us that Jesus Christ, as God, is the source of all light and that in Him there is *"no darkness at all."*[27]

Our feelings may grow dark from time to time in different phases of life, but if we're believers in Christ then darkness is an oppression from outside us, not real darkness within. In Chapter four we talked about the holiness of our bodies because they are temples of

---

[26] John 1:4-5 RSV

[27] 1 John 1:5 RSV

the living God. It's the great mystery of faith in Christ that we don't just believe with our minds, we actually have Christ living within us. St. Paul affirms this in his letter to the Galatians…

> *I have been crucified with Christ; it is no longer I who live,* **Christ who lives in me**; *and the life I now live in the flesh I live by faith in the Son of God, who loved me and gave himself for me.*[28] (Emphasis added)

When our feelings grow dark through grief and loss hopelessness begins to set in. If left unanswered our feelings of hopelessness can be extremely dangerous. We run the risk of losing all hope. We must counter such feelings with truth and light. The truth that Jesus is the light in our lives and that no darkness can overcome Him gives us hope. We remind ourselves of the truth that God loves us, and that through Christ we can conquer all things that come against us.[29]

How do we find hope in the midst of great darkness, even in the face of the death of our loved ones? We remind ourselves of the promises of God. We set our hearts on eternal things which are unseen because we know all that is seen is temporary and fading away.

> *So we do not lose heart. Though our outer nature is wasting away, our inner nature is being renewed every*

---

[28] Galatians 2:20 RSV

[29] Philippians 4:13 RSV

> *day. For this slight momentary affliction is preparing for us an eternal weight of glory beyond all comparison, because we look not to the things that are seen but to the things that are unseen; for the things that are seen are transient, but the things that are unseen are eternal.*
>
> -2 Corinthians 4:16-18

When the anxiety of hopelessness begins to surround you, you must do as it says in 1 Peter 5:7 *"Cast all your anxiety on Him, for He cares about you."* The Book of Hebrews reminds us the Jesus Christ is the same yesterday, today, and forever.[30] As such, we know we can always count on Him to help us clear away the dark clouds of our grief. Often, His help comes though the incarnational living of a friend or through a counselor or pastor. We must avail ourselves of all the help there is in our modern world. We are very blessed to live in such a time when help is so readily available.

We must also remember that as we seek help in others, the true source of all light is Jesus Christ. He is the way, the truth, and the life.[31] All truth is His truth, and ultimately all help his from Him.

God cares for our grief. He doesn't want us to be lost in the dark of our own fears and heartaches. When you find yourself lost in grief, remember you're never alone, and the One who is with you always, cares.

---

[30] Hebrews 13:8 RSV

[31] John 14:6 RSV

When loss and grief come, He's right there with you, hurting with you and comforting you. He's helping you to find hope in the face of death.

God is not just some being far away in Heaven. He is the One who loves you more than anyone else. He is the One who knows you better than anyone else. He is the One who made you, and no matter how alone you feel, He is right there with you. In fact, He is IN you. He is a presence in the dark you can always count on to bring hope… even in the face of death.

EPILOGUE

Now that you've taken time to read and think about death, perhaps more than you've ever done before, I want you to consider taking some very important and very practical steps toward facing the reality of your own death. I'd also like you to hear the story of my friend and colleague, Billy Byler. At the end of this Epilogue I've included an open letter from Billy to you. In it he shares his story of grief, and how the incarnational love of others, as well as the love of God became for him – a presence in the dark.

One of the greatest gifts you can give to your loved ones is to prepare for your own death. The more prepared you are to face death the better your family will do when the grief of your passing settles in. There are three steps I want you to consider.

These steps are not necessarily in order of importance. Everyone is at a different place along the journey. However, it's been my experience, in almost twenty years of ministry, that most of us need to spend time on all three.

First Step: Be sure you have enough life insurance. I know that no one likes to think about life insurance; they like paying for it even less. But, while money can't buy feelings, it is a tool to be used. And, when used properly I know of no greater tool to help deal the pain of loss than an adequate amount of insurance to relieve the financial burden death can bring. Your family having to face your death is hard enough, but having to face it and not knowing how they will pay for your funeral is worse – much worse.

I can't tell you how many funerals I've done where the family wasn't financially prepared to pay for a funeral and burial. Seeing that pain and strain added on top of their grief just seems cruel. I know their loved one didn't mean to be cruel by not being prepared, but that's what it felt like to those left to bear the load.

According to the **National Funeral Directors Association** statistics[32], the median cost of a funeral service in 2014, with burial and a vault was $8058.00. That doesn't count the costs for burial site, monument or marker, and other miscellaneous expenses. These can easily add an additional $2000.00. While Cremation costs are less than traditional burial, there are still many factors to be considered, and the sudden expense of a few thousand dollars can create a great strain for families. Such strains often cause them to make decisions based on cost rather than need.

Additionally, there's more than just finances to

---

[32] http://www.nfda.org/news/statistics

consider. The planning of a Service of Remembrance is also very important. The service is a critical element in helping your family to grieve healthily. After all is said and done, don't you want your family to have the peace of mind of knowing that whenever your death comes, they won't have to make lots of decisions and worry about how to care for your final expenses?

Second Step: Begin planning for your death. Again, the National Funeral Directors Association has many resources to help in your planning. You'll find their consumer resources page has a complete list of what you'll need to do. There's a lot more to think about than most people realize in making funeral arrangements. You'll find their resources will guide you through all the necessary steps so you don't forget anything. Remember, you are giving your family an immeasurable gift by doing this pre-planning.

Additionally, they also have a wonderful resource called *"Have the Talk of A Lifetime"* that will help you begin the discussion of how to be sure your family knows your wishes and what to do when the time of your death comes. The booklet is available in a downloadable pdf. Download it today and begin talking about your future needs and plans.

Third Step: Take time to consider your beliefs about life and death. I have written many things from a Christian perspective. However, I know not everyone reading this book is a Christian. In fact, I hope many who are not Christian will read this book because there is something for every life on these pages.

As I stated earlier in the book, it doesn't matter to me what a person's faith is, if any, when I'm invited to help a family with a funeral. I believe all life is sacred and all people deserve the dignity of a proper burial or memorial service through which to be remembered. Every family deserves the comfort that comes from a service of remembrance and having someone come along-side them in their mourning.

If you've been offended in any way by my thoughts in this book, please forgive me. My intention is never to judge anyone for their beliefs. My faith as a Christian is invaluable to me. However, I know many people who've been emotionally hurt by people and churches who claimed to be Christian. Sadly, those hurts kept them from recognizing what I believe are essential truths of life, death, and the world to come.

I make no recommendations to you about choosing one church or denomination over another. I only ask that if you are one who's been hurt by what I would consider a false Christian spirit, then on behalf of the God of our creation who called us all into being, and who will one day call us all home, please accept my apology.

By writing this book, I only wish to show you the love of my God and savior, Jesus Christ, who has called me to tell you how much He loves you. I trust your eternal state to Him who is too wise to do wrong and too good to make a mistake – the only wise God of the Universe. May God's blessing be upon you and remain with you, now and forever and to the ages of ages.

Amen.

Prayerfully,
Christ's Merciful Servant,

Brad Riley

AN OPEN LETTER FROM A FRIEND

After a three-year battle with liver cancer, my wife passed away at the age of 24. We were two months shy of our second anniversary. The grief was overwhelming. No one knew what I felt. Sure, others knew her and grieved the loss, but I alone stood as a 25-year-old widower. Nothing felt right anymore. This wasn't how my life was supposed to turn out. I didn't doubt God's existence, but I doubted His motives, plans and logic. I cried out to Him, yelled at Him and argued with Him through many sleepless nights. It didn't make sense, and I felt like no one else knew what I was going through. The darkness was overwhelming.

Praise God for the people of my local church. They loved on me, cared for me, fed me and checked in on me. My pastor didn't try to push complex theological discussions on me to answer all my doubts. He just called up to tell me he was thinking about me. An older couple at church didn't try to fix my loneliness with introductions to single friends that could replace my lost relationship. They just invited me over for dinner and to watch college football. When I wasn't at church because of an out-of-town trip, I'd get a card or text message letting me know I was missed.

These people offered no answers, no fixes and no pressure to move on. They only offered care. And it was exactly what I needed.

I'm so thankful for my church family at Midland Valley Community Church. As I wrestled, argued and complained to God about the woeful situation that He, at worst, caused and, at best, allowed, He spent that time working through His people – my church – to bring me care, love and companionship that I didn't even know I needed. Community has been so important in my journey through grief. When grief found me, I found a body of believers who carried me when going through life alone was an impossibility.

Years later, Jon and Tim Foreman of the band *Switchfoot* wrote these words for a song called "The Day That I Found God." This describes my journey beautifully:

> *I found strength but it wasn't what I thought I found peace in the places I forgot I found riches ain't the things that I had bought I found out The day I lost myself was the day that I found God.*[33]

Rev. Billy Byler
Young Adults Pastor
First Church of the Nazarene
Wichita, Kansas

---

[33] Foreman, Jon. "The Day That I Found God." *Where the Light Shines Through*, Switchfoot, 2016.

ABOUT THE AUTHOR

Brad Riley is an ordained minister in the Church of the Nazarene. With a Catholic background from his youth, his heritage gives him an appreciation for the historic Christian faith. As a minister he loves all branches of Christianity. A good friend has coined a new name for him... *"Orthocathorene"*; part Orthodox, part Catholic, and part Nazarene. He takes that as a high compliment.

Brad's work in the community often opens up opportunities to minister in ecumenical settings where he meets with families from various to no theological backgrounds. What really matters to those families is not his denomination or creed, but that he shares the love of Jesus with them in some of their most difficult times.

Brad and his wife Rhonda have served churches in San Antonio, Texas and Wichita, Kansas. They have been married for 31 years and have two children. They reside in Wichita, Kansas, where he currently serves as Associate and Teaching Pastor of the First Church of the Nazarene. He is also the founder of The Merciful Servants of Christ, a discipleship order for spiritual formation, and The Ecumenical Christian Prayer Group. Brad also travels to speak in churches and organizations inspiring them to grow deeper as intentional disciples of Jesus Christ.

Made in the USA
Lexington, KY
02 February 2018